BUSINESS

BREAKTH

ROUGH

IDEAS

**DISCOVER SECRETS THAT YOU CAN USE TO MAKE YOUR
BUSINESS AND YOUR LIFE A SUCCESS**

ISAAC GIWA

BUSINESS BREAKTHROUGH IDEAS

Published by

ISGIBSON SERVICES

6, kamoru Adeyemi Street, Ire-Akari Estate, Isolo, Lagos-Nigeria.

P.O. Box 621, Ikeja

Lagos, Nigeria

Tel: 234-1-8023147715

234-1-8036665662

E-mail: isgibsonservices@gmail.com

isaacgiwabooks@gmail.com

NB: All scripture quotations are from the King James Version of the Bible, except otherwise stated.

CONTENTS

1

WISDOM FOR BUSINESS BREAKTHROUGH

Make wisdom your provision for the journey from youth to old age, for it is a more certain support than all other possessions. – Bias

As a business man, if there is anything that you must seek after, it is wisdom. It is a major course you must pass to succeed in the school of business success.

To be successful in business, you need the wisdom of God.

Wisdom is a supernatural understanding of a situation from God's point of view. It is understanding the "how" of events.

Wisdom is a major asset which guarantees successful business. If someone lacks wisdom in his business, he begins to struggle and engage in trial and error.

There is no obstacle in your life and business you cannot overcome, no problem you cannot solve, and no goal you cannot achieve by applying the force of wisdom to your situation.

Every crisis you might face in business is a wisdom issue. Wisdom is the baseline for a successful business life. It is the quality of wisdom at work in any business that determines the quality of results obtainable. The quality of wisdom applied determines the quality of result expected.

STRATEGIC THINKING

Thinking is exercising your mind.

We think to generate wisdom and answer to the challenges of life.

Thinking helps you to generate answers to the pulses and problems of business life.

The brain is meant for working and until you work it, nothing works.

Brain Tracy, A Business Guru, once said, **energy and imagination are the greatest asset in business.** The farther you think, the farther you go. Only thinking business moves forward.

There is something that instigates thinking and that thing is called problem. What problem does is to touch on those mental cells so that they can scatter in order to go and locate the answers where they are hidden.

Problem creates mental reaction. Do you know you think better when you are under pressure. Don't dodge your problems rather confront them. Give your problem a mental arrest.

A STRONG KNOWLEDGE BASE

Wisdom is the accurate application of knowledge. There is no wise man until there is a knowledgeable man. Knowledge is the principal raw materials for wisdom. It is your wealth of knowledge that determines your weight of wisdom.

When Solomon in the bible lost his taste for knowledge, his wisdom was eroded. When you stop learning, you stop growing, your security in the school of wisdom is a strong knowledge base. It is your references that give credence to your thought.

Every truly wise person is a committed learner. The reason why many readers are not wise is that many don't know that you acquire knowledge by reading, and you process the knowledge you have acquired into wisdom by thinking. Therefore, it is not enough to be a reader, you must be a thinking reader. Meditation is the gateway to a world of wisdom.

"I don't divide the world into the weak and strong or the successes and failures and those who make it or those who don't". I divide the world into learners and non-learners". – Benjamin Barber

2

THE FORCE OF CREATIVITY

Creative thinking involves breaking out of established patterns in order to look at things in different ways – Edward De Bond

Business success is a product of creativity. Your ability to be creative will determine the level of success you will enjoy.

Creativity is the ability of creating things. That is, the ability to generate idea that will enable you to solve problems, overcome obstacles and achieve your goal. Napoleon Hill once said, "whatever the mind can conceive and believe, it can achieve.

Your mind is designed in such a way that you cannot have an idea on one hand without having the power and ability to bring that idea into reality on the other hand.

Your ability to develop ideas and be creative in life and business is unlimited. This means that your ability to succeed is unlimited as well.

INNOVATING AND INVENTING

Through creativity and innovation, you must devised betters ways of doing the tasks your community had undertaken for years. When you find a better way of doing things, it will place you in a position of great advantage over people who still held on to the old slow and tired method.

Learn to be a person dreams, imagination, innovation and creativity. Let your brain be always ticking with new ideas and possibilities. Doing the same old thing will not get the results needed for business success.

Create new wealth by wisely investing the little you have. Embrace time as a friend and work patiently toward financial fortune. Be creator of wealth. Focus on nurturing and cultivating the little you have into abundance. Do not wait for success to happen by itself; create success.

Business success and expansion are by product of new ways of thinking and doing things.

THINK OUTSIDE OF THE BOX

Your creativity ability is activated and provoked by three factors, your passion; second, pressing problems; and third, focused question. The more you focus your mind on achieving your business objectives, solving your problems or answering the tough question about your business and personal life, the more creative you become and the better your mind works for you in the future.

There is always a way out of every business challenges. creativity is the key. Be creative. Be inventive and imaginative and you will experience business breakthrough. Most of the big companies you see today did not start where they are now; it is creativity and continuous innovation that brought them to the lime light.

Always learn to come up with an idea or strategy to improve your business and your work. Always find newer, better, faster, cheaper and easier ways to accomplish a result. That is what creativity is all about. Don't go for status quo, think outside the box.

BECOMING A CREATIVE WORKER

Isaac in the bible was a creative worker. He was a highly creative man. where he was sojourning, there had been famine in the land while others were complaining, suffering and waiting for the arrival of rain; Isaac set himself down and thought of the way he could get water to feed his flocks and for his farm, then the idea of digging a well came to him and he prospered during famine.**(Genesis 26: 12-13)**

Jacob too was a creative person, he used the creative ability in Him to prevent his father-in-law from cheating him after serving for several years. He devised a way to make the goats and cattle he is given to mate before some trees of particular design, when the goats and cattle conceived, they gave birth to young ones that looked like the pattern of those trees. So he ends up being a successful business man.

Wherever you are, whatever you are dong, whatever your situation and circumstance is, you have creative ability; in form of an infinite ability to generate unusual ideas, to solve any problem and achieve any goals.

Have you ever wondered how the Japanese were able to rise from the ruins of the Second World War to become the great economic power of today? The Japanese didn't invent the computer. They didn't invent the car, camera, the television the fridge, the air-conditioner, the washing machine, the vacuum cleaner, the photo film. In fact they didn't invent a lot of this, what they did was they just copied, refined and improved on the existing products. They actually just used their creative ability on the same product but see how successful they have become in business

3

BE SUPREMELY CONFIDENT

Go confidently in the direction of your dreams. Live the life you've imagined – Henry David Thoreau

Starting and running a business is not a job for the coward. You need a lion and a daring heart to have a lion share in the market place. Therefore, no confidence, no achievement, no reward.

You need a bold heart for a bold step. Behind every outstanding accomplishment in the market place is confidence. Talent and potential will not produce until backed up with confidence.

Be daring
Confidence is champion's backbone. It is one thing to have talent and another thing to turn it loose; confidence is the switch that turns your potential loose.

Successful business people have the confidence to make decisions and to take action in the face of fear and uncertainty, with no guarantee of success. Your ability to launch into the deep, to step out in faith, even when there is a chance of failure and loss, is the mark of true greatness.

Someone wise said, "No man's success or health will never reach beyond his own confidence; as a rule, we erect our own barriers.

THE TRAP OF FEAR

It is impossible for the fearful and fainthearted to accomplish great things in business. Such people will be afraid to take on new and unfamiliar in order to create new product and service. The numerous "giants of impossibilities" along the way will easily intimidate them".

Fear paralyses; Do not allow it to prevent you from moving forward in life and business.

Do not allow anything to intimidate you as you move on towards the realization of your vision. If you want to accomplish great things in business, you must not turn away from the lions and giants that lie on the way. Don't allow the fear of criticism and the fear of failure to stop you from achieving your vision. Brain Tracy wrote in his best selling book, the 100 absolutely unbreakable laws of business success that, "Every great success is preceded by many failures and accompanied by countless criticism".

DEVELOP A WELL ABLE MENTALITY

Business success has eluded many today because they see it as unattainable and impossible. You need a sense of ability to accomplish great feat in business.

To succeed in business, always have the right perspective, with the right mentality, you are able to see that there is nothing in the matter before you.

Every obstacle in business is a potential new product or service, all you need to do is to confront it.

In 1904, after so much frustrated efforts had gone into trying to make a vessel flying the air, scientist met in London and concluded that it as impossible for any piece of metal to fly on the air. But two brothers (the Wright Brothers) despised this conclusion and kept on at their experiment. And in 1910, they proved the scientists wrong by flying the first machine in the air!.

4

DEVELOP BUSINESS SKILL

Our main business is not what lies dimly of a distance, but to do what lies clearly at hand effectively and efficiently. – Thomas Url

Every great and successful business venture thrives on skill; lack of skill can kill any business.

Skill connotes know how

It means expertise

It is the force behind outstanding business success

Every business is at the mercy of skill

There are some facts about your business. And these facts must be consciously acquired and intelligently applied for you to make wonderful profit in your business activities.

In the business world, only excellence is celebrated and it takes skill to arrive at excellence.

Someone wisely said,

"If you can become very good at what you do, there is nothing that can stop you from getting paid more and promoted faster".

Dear reader, you can rescue that your business that is about to crash by going after relevant knowledge that will boost your business.

MULTIPLY YOUR SUCCESS

You have to learn the skill of your trade. You must constantly ask your self this questions; what one skill, if I develop and did in an excellent fashion, would have the greatest positive impact on my business?

Once you are clear about the one skill that can help you the most, set the acquisition of this skill as a goal, write it down, make it plain, and then work to getting better in this area every single day because lack of skill can kill your business dream.

And remember this; nobody is going to pay you for your talent and your gift. People will always pay you for your skill. Skill is adding training to your talent. many people are talented but untrained talented people. But before your talent can profit you, it must have skill and skill is knowledge.

When you have skill, you use less time to achieve much in business but when you don't have skill you will achieve a little. If you desire to take charge of your finances and your business, you must be skilled in managing your finances.

Skill will reduce your sweat and multiply your business. Education or degree should not be mistaken for skill, skill must be acquired or your dream business will be killed.

QUALITY PRODUCTS & SERVICES

Someone rightly said,

"If a man would write a better book, preach a better sermon, make a better mouse trap, than his neighbour, though he builds his house in the wood, the world will make beaten paths to his door".

Successful businesses are constantly striving for excellence and improvement.
Excellence means a skillful approach to a given task.

The quality of your product and services will make people find your company.
The skillful design of your clothes for examples as a fashion designer will make all admirers of beautiful clothing find your shop. The efficiency of your latest marketing strategies will make the whole world abandon the old one and rush for yours. Your excellent oriented business environment will attract a large number of customers.

The undoing of many businesses today is un-skillfulness.
It is time to go for fact. it is time to buy books and audio and video program. Read all the magazines in your area of business. Read and study the latest books. Attend courses and seminars given by experts in your area of business.

HOW TO DEVELOP BUSINESS SKILL

It is principally by training.

It is not just enough for you to be in business.

You must also be trained for what you are doing.

Training will increase your ability to prosper and be productive in all that you do.

In the world we live in, training is extremely crucial. In the aero industry, major airlines require that their pilots, regardless of how long they have been flying undergo fresh training, at least twice a year to maintain and also develop their skills. Similarly, big companies and organisation that are doing well today invest a great deal in seminars and workshops that would help upgrade and refine the skills of their staff.

For your business to enjoy unlimited success, training is not a choice it is a must. Don't assume it, go for it.

Skill is a trade you learn from practitioner. It has to be acquired through training from those who have it.

One thing that has contributed to my success today is that I take my time to learn from those who have gone ahead of me.

Dear reader, there is no level of gift or talent that is substitute for training because in every thing you will ever do well; you will have to learn it.

5

SECRETS OF BUSINESS PROGRESS

There are no such things as limits to growth because there are no limits on the human capacity for intelligence, imagination and wonder. – Ronald Reagan

Stagnation is failure. Someone who remaining on one spot is actually going backward without knowing. Failure is quick to catch up with such person and overtake those who are not making steady progress in business.

It is not a sin to start small but it is a sin punishable by slow death to remain small. No matter the level of success you have experience in the time past, if you are not advancing and progressing, you are dying.

Bill Gates turned around the face of the computer industry via the principle of business progress and improvement.

The initial versions of the graphic – based operating system, "windows", which his company developed were commercial failures and also full of bugs.

However, Bill Gates continued to develop himself and Microsoft continued to improve by correcting the bugs until window 3:1 version, which achieved considerable success. The next version was released after Windows 95, which recorded tremendous commercial success because it was a great improvement over the previous version.

Business progress and improvement is your guarantee for continuous and unlimited business success.

Dear reader, I want to encourage you to avoid the syndrome of "success destination disease". That is the, "I have arrived attitude". As long as you are green, you are growing but as soon as you arrive, you will start to rot.

For you to survive, thrive and succeed in a fast changing world, you will have to get back to the drawing board to find new ways to do what you are doing faster and better and also to carry out research to make your system of operation more efficient. You will have to study and learn aggressively how to enlarge your marketing potentials by penetrating new markets and how to increase your income base.

After only five years of operation, the ford company belonging to Henry Ford was producing six thousand one hundred and eighty-one cars in a year. But he was not satisfied with this result. A few years after so many research and discovery, the company adopted a revolutionary assembly line method and soon produced thirty five thousand, model T Ford cars a year. Not too long after that, Ford factories throughout the world were building four thousand cars a day.

Take practical steps on how to grow big and make progress, making progress in business involves 4 major steps.

BASIC REQUIREMENT FOR BUSINESS PROGRESS

1.   **Forgetting those things that are behind.** Many people are unduly attached to the past, when you refuse to move beyond yesterday, you cannot advance into great future that lies ahead of you. To make business progress, you must let go of what is behind. Not just past failures, but your past successes too. Do not dwell on your past successes, move on. Do not allow yesterday's failure to limit you either. Each new day brings along with it fresh opportunities to try again.

When you are locked up in the past, you are incapacitated, but when you choose to put the past behind you, you are released to explore new frontiers, you are ready to access greater things.

2.   **Reaching forth**

That is dealing with your present challenges.
There is no challenge on your path that is superior to your mind power. No challenge is bigger than you, nothing is too strong to defeat you.

3.   **Focusing on the future**

Your future is your picture.
The happiest people are those who live in their future. No matter where you are now; no matter where you have been before, there is always something greater ahead, there is always a higher level of opportunities, there is always a higher quality of life.

4.   **Learn to press (pursuit)**

You cannot enjoy business progress until you press to it; everything precious comes out of pressure.

If you dodge the pressure, you miss the precious. Pressing is the price for business progress.

Always shun short-cuts, there is no short cut to destiny, every short cut always leads to a dead end. The shortest route between two points is a straight line not a short cut.

Nothing happens until you do something.

The longest journey is one step after the other.

Vision is of no value without pursuit

Pursuit is what gives vision value.

Pursuit is the relevant force that transforms your business vision into reality.

Martin Luther King Jnr. Said, **"if you cannot fly, run, if you can run, walk; if you cannot walk, then crawl. By all means, keep moving". I have kept moving!**

6

HAVE A GOOD CUSTOMER SERVICE

The single most important thing is to focus obsessively on the customer...our goal is to be the earth's most customers
– Centric Company
– Jeff Bezos (Founder amazon.com)

As far as the market is concerned, the customer is the KING. Today customers expect excellence in service. If they sense that you are not putting them first they will feel disappointed. Your reward and compensation in life and business is in direct proportion to the value of service that you give to others.

The foundation of every business success is commitment to quality customer service. Your commitment to service is what guaranteed your success. Everyone who is committed to solving a particular problem is a candidate of success. If you will be service driven, outstanding business will be guaranteed. Until you are disposed to service mankind, success is not view.

All great fortune begin with the sale of personal service. There are many self made millionaires in our environment today. Many started in life without no money, no formal education, and no family connection. But they all excel in life by finding a way to serve others more effectively. Don't ever stop improving on the quality of service that you give to others.

Don't labor to make money but labour to service the need of mankind and money will come to you.

Nothing guarantees true and enduring success like a quality service.

Be committed to service and success will be waiting for you. Be your best in wherever you are, that is the way to get to where you are going.

The most successful men and women in our society are those who are able to "lose themselves" in serving the people who depend upon them for what they do.

INCREASE YOUR VALUE

The quality of your product and services are the deciding factor on how much your business is valued by the world. If you desire to increase your success in business begin to increase the value of your customer service.

Increase the quality of product and services you are offering to the market. Strive to be the best in customer services in your business career.

If you want to make money give good service. – Mike Ferry.

7
NEVER GIVE UP ON YOUR BUSINESSES IDEA

Thoroughness characterizes all successful men. Genius is the art of taking infinite pains... all great achievement has been characterized by extreme care, infinite painstaking, even to the minutest detail.   – Elbert Hubbard

Persistence is the iron quality of outstanding businesses success. For you to experience outstanding business achievement you need to develop an attitude of not giving up on your ideas and pursuit until you get your desired result. Keep on keeping on; keep on pursuing your dream, if you try long enough, its likely to work.

Persistence is the act of tireless pursuit. For you to experience enduring success in business, you need to learn to keep at your businesses goal despite all odds and challenges. Persistence and perseverance gives motion to accomplishment.

Hit and run never wins a prize, it is hit and stick that wins. No precious things in life begin in fullness; every precious thing must begin small. Every tree no matter how big begins as a seed. So don't despite the day of little beginning, it is ordained of God that everything starts as a baby then grow into maturity.

Persistence enables you to keep moving. There is a due season for everything, many people fail in the way of pursuit for lack of persistence.

Business life is in phases. Agree with the phase you are per time and keep moving.

In your bid in pursuit, don't mind the mockers, don't get distracted. Because if you mind the mockers, you can't get to your destination. When you back your businesses idea with unshakable persistence, you will find out that there is nothing in the world that can stop you.

BULLDOG TENACITY

Sir Winston Churchill believed, and proved and again throughout his life time, that bulldog tenacity in the face of what appeared to be over-whelming defeat was often the quality that turned that defeat into victory. He once said, never, ever, ever give up".

Consider Abraham Lincoln, he became one of the best president in American history. But the achievement didn't come until he had passed through many difficulties and challenges. Born in the back woods of Kentucky in 1809, Lincoln work as a rail splitter, flatboat man, storekeeper, postmaster and surveyor before he become a lawyer. Altogether Lincoln's formal education added up to about a year.

He is a classic case of bulldog tenacity. failed in businesses in1831, defeated in legislature in 1832; again failed in businesses in 1833,had nervous breakdown in 1834, defeated running for speaker in 1838, defeated running for post of elector in 1840, defeated running for congress in 1843, elected to congress in 1846, defeated running for congress in 1848, defeated running for senate in 1855, defeated running for vice president in 1856, defeated running for senate in 1858.

Finally, in 1860 he was elected as the 16th and one of the greatest presidents in America history, if Abraham Lincoln had given up after he had failed several time in politics, America would have been robbed of the unparallel leadership of their greatest president.

Consider one of the greatest political comeback ever staged in history was that of Richard Nixon. He was defeated by John F. Kennedy for the presidency of the United States in 1962. His subsequent defeat in the campaign for the governorship of his native California in 1962 all but wrote him off in the minds of most observers. Not so with Richard Nixon, with bulldog tenacity, he held on to his dream of the white house, he became the 37th President of the United States.

CHINESE BAMBOO

In the far East, the people plant a tree called the Chinese Bamboo.During the first four years, they water and fertilize the plant with seemingly little or no results. Then the fifth year, they again apply water and fertilizer and in five weeks time the tree grows ninety feet in height. The obvious questions is; did the Chinese bamboo tree grew in five years? The answer is, it grew ninety feet in five years. Because if at any time during those five years the people had stopped watering and fertilizing the tree, it would have died.

Many times our dreams and ideas appear not to be succeeding, we are tempted to give up and quit trying. Instead, we need to continue to water and fertilize those dream and ideas, nurturing the seeds of the vision God has placed within us. Because if you do not quit, if you display perseverance and endurance, you will also reap a great harvest.

A man who met a business Guru Master on the road asked, "which way is success"? The bearded sage doesn't speak but instead point, to a place off in the distance.

The man, thrilled by the prospect of quick and easy success, rushes off in the appropriate direction. Splat! He limps back, bruised and stunned, assuming he must have misinterpreted the message.

He repeats his question to the Guru, who again points silently in the same direction.

He obediently walks off once more, this time the splat is deafening, and when he crawls back, he is bloody, broken and irate. "I asked you which way is success!" He screamed at the Guru. "I followed the direction you indicated! And all I got was splattered! No more of the pointing! Talk!

Only then does the Guru speak, "success is that way. Just a little after the splat". You find this principle of persistence, of keeping on, in the life and business of countless great men and women. John D. Rockefeller, at one time the richest self made man in the world, wrote", I do not think there is any other quality so essential to success of any kind, as the quality for perseverance, it overcomes almost everything, even nature".

8

GOING THE EXTRA-MILE

Always do more than you're paid for or you'll never be paid much more than you're getting now.
– Earl Nightingale

Great achievers and successful business go the extra mile. if you consistently do more than what you are expected or paid to do – whether you are a professional businessman, an executive or an entrepreneur, you will eventually be compensated for far more than you do.

Achieving great height in business is not really easy. Reaching the top of any field is difficult, time consuming and often tedious. The reason it isn't crowded at the top is because many give up too soon. They are too willing to give up when the going gets tough.
Successful business people prevailed because they refused to quit, they continued to toil alone along after the masses had given up and gone home.

The Wright Brother should not have been the first to achieve flight in an airplane. But the man destined to do it gave up before he achieved his dream. He refused to go to the extra-mile. Even though, he is an accomplished thinker, scientist, and inventor. He has published several important works on aerodynamics, and possessed a vision for achieving manned flight. But he died as a failure. Two years after his failed attempt to fly an airplane, he abandoned his experiments. He suffered a stroke and a year after he died. But the Wright Brothers, the bicycle mechanics who pioneered manned flight in the first part of the twentieth century, with no university education were not even the leaders in aviation industry.

They achieved great success because of their willingness to go the extra-mile. And today, while even young school children have heard of the Wright brothers, no one remembered the other scientist even his name. **"The difference between ordinary and extra ordinary is that little extra". – Zig Ziglar**

Financial wealth is only one measure of success. The truly happy and successful individual is the man or woman who is mentally sound, emotionally stable, financially secure, challenged in his or her career, and is making a difference in the lives of others. For a person to enjoy outstanding success, he or she must be willing to do more than what he or she is presently doing. If you are not too big for your current position, then you are too small for it. Outgrow your current position to enjoy great success.

If you do more than you are paid for, you will be paid for – more than you are doing. Don't limit what you are willing to do. learn to go the extra mile. **"It's not that I'm so smart, it's just that I stay with problems longer". – Albert Einstein.**

Napoleon Hill found that key quality of successful business people, most of whom started at the bottom, many of them penniless, was that early in life; they developed the habit of "going the extra mile". They discovered, as the old saying goes, that "there are never any traffic jams on the extra mile. Your success in life and business will be in direct proportion to what you do after you do what you are expected to do".

"People who never do any more than they get paid for never get paid for any more than they do" – Albert Hubbard.

9

UNDERSTANDING BUSINESS MANAGEMENT

Management is the skillful use of various resources to accomplish the purpose of an organization. It is the judicial or sensible use of material or people, time and finances to accomplish defined objective, purpose or goal of a business organization.

Management can also be defined as the effective placement of men to perform certain responsibilities in an organization. Any business giant that goes on alone will end up as a victim.

Goliath of Gath in the Bible went out alone, he paid with his life. Management is ordained by God to preserve your life and business. The reason why many businesses and great business people fail or bankrupt is because they did not take the subject of management very serious.

BASIC PRINCIPLE THAT GUIDES BUSINESS MANAGEMENT

1.   A Clear Goal

An effective business management must establish definite objective or goals. these could be long term or short term. The long term goal is the overall goal while the short time goal is the given task and objectives that will help achieve the long term goal.

Successful business people think about their goals most of the time, as a result, they are continually moving towards their goals and their goals are continually moving toward them.

2.   *Motivation*

Motivation is the art of stirring up or stimulating your business team or staff interest to accomplish a stipulated task. It also means wetting their appetite to do the task; it is the will to act.

Learn how to recognize, praise and show love to people working for you as subordinates. By doing so, they will become better motivated to accomplish great things. Many people can organize, but it does not matter how well your business is organized, if the people around you are not motivated; the business will end up in failure. A business that is motivated is a business that is alive; it is one that has life.

3.   **Effective Communication & Relationship**

This has to do with how to get the best by fostering and by encouraging good relationship between staffs and management. There must be cordial relationship; there must be effective dissemination of information in the system.

Be aware of office politics, and set an example by never taking part yourself. If staff become involved in political games, intervene quickly, make it clear that nobody will win from the exchange and insist that differences are settle.

You should regularly take time to talk with each member of your staff. Ask them if anything would make their job easier and try your best to fulfill requests. There must be a cordial relationship to enjoy effective business management.

4.   Authority

Authority has to do with the power to give order; not only this but also the power to make them comply with a given order. Power is the ability to do things.

Effective management must have the ability to make rules and regulation towards the fulfillment of the business objectives. And management must also have the power to enforce the rule.

5.   Responsibility

Responsibility means response to ability or ability to respond. It has to do with been answerable for the discharge of a particular duty or assignment. Management must have in mind that it is answerable to a particular assignment.

6.   Delegation

This is the act of giving somebody a right and freedom to perform a particular assignment on behalf of the management.

Every business requires men to stand with you to run. Business is not just having an idea; it also involves raising men to run the idea.

Delegation is the sharing of responsibility and authority with others by entrusting them with certain assignment.

Delegation practically means to be assigned and be empowered. Business vision becomes realistic through people, principally by DELEGATION.

7.   The Principle Of Division Of Labor

It has to do with dividing the entire assignment into small bit or unit and assign this small unit to individuals for execution.

OTHER BOOKS BY ISAAC GIWA.

1.   Million dollar generating habit

2.   Digging your diamond mine

3.   Your mind is a miracle

4.   Be a super achiever

5.   Provoking your harvest

6.   Seizing the moment

7.   Secrets of financial success

8.   Changing your world

9.   Get ready...money cometh

10.   Secrets for business success

11.   Simple ideas on how to create your own miracle

GET CONNECTED

God is our power source.

He is the well-spring of wisdom. Once He comes into your heart a profound relationship with wisdom and power becomes inevitable. He is the foundation of grace. Without the flow of his divine grace, we malfunction and life becomes tedious. His graceful support is still available for you today.

He wants to help you in achieving your dreams and desires in life. He has helped many others. He can help you. So, my friends you too can enjoy his remarkable support today!

All you need to do is to accept Him as your Lord and Saviour. You will experience a change in your heart.

Say this prayer with me right now:

"Lord Jesus, thank you for dying for me on the cross". I turn to you to establish a relationship with you today. I ask that you forgive me my sins and cleanse me with your previous blood.

Let your life, grace and wisdom begin to find fulfillment. In my life today. Rule in my heart today as my Lord and personal Saviour.

Thank you for saving me.

OUR MISSION

- To let you know that God wants you to prosper and succeed.

- To help you discover the tremendous potential the creator has graciously invested in your life.

- To impact into your life the manifold wisdom of God.

- To ensure your total deliverance from failure and poverty.

- To release through effective prayer, the power of God to effect positive change in your circumstances.

YOUR LETTER IS VERY IMPORTANT TO ME

You are a special person to me and I believe that you are special to God.

I want to help you in any way possible. Do you have any prayer request? Write me when you need an intercessor to pray for you.

Let be hear from you when you are facing spiritual needs or experiencing a conflict in your business, marriage and career.

When you write, my staff and I will pray over your letter. I will write you back to help you receive the miracle you need.

I will look forward to your letter.

For more information, please contact;

ISAAC GIWA

Wisdom Impartation Ministries Int'l

P.O. box 621, Ikeja, Lagos-Nigeria.

Phone: 234-802-314-7715, 234-803-666-5662

E-Mail: wisdomimpart@yahoo.com

isaacgiwabooks@gmail..com

WILL YOU BECOME A PARTNER WITH MY MINISTRY?

Your Financial Seeds Are So Powerful In Helping Heal Broken Lives. When You Sow Into the Work of God, Miracle Harvest Are Guaranteed

*Supernatural protection. (Malachi 3:10)

*Supernatural favour (Luke 6:38)

*Supernatural Health (Isaiah (58:8)

*Supernatural wisdom & financial ideas. (Deuteronomy 8:18)

Sow your seed today, then focus your expectation for the 100 - fold return! An unusual seed will always create an unusual harvest.

To Sow Your Seed Today

Pay Into Any:

Bank: Guarantee Trust Bank

Account Name: Isaac Giwa

Account Number: 0006808883

Or Call,

+234-8023147715

+234-8036665662

+234-8189800366

E-Mail: wisdomimpart@yahoo.com

P.O. Box 621, Ikeja, Lagos, Nigeria.

BOOK ENCOUNTERS

A lot of people have received their breakthroughs just by reading Dr. Isaac Giwa's books. His books are life-changing manual and anointed spiritual weapons with which many fought battles over Failure, Stagnation, Poverty, Hardship, Afflictions e.t.c., and won!

Read these:

The book "Money Cometh" has done wonders to my finances. I recommend it for anyone that wants to succeed in this peculiar environment of Africa. It's a must read.

Olayinka Aina, Author:

Enjoy A Superb Service Year"

Lagos-Nigeria

Your book is an inspiring one and very intellectual. It has taught me how to be wise financially.

Josephine Asare, Author:

"All About Your Dreams

Accra-Ghana

I have read your book titled "secret of BUSINESS SUCCESS" I found the book quite educative, informative and above all it's a book that anybody that wants to succeed in business need to go through.

-Hassan Yusuf

Kaduna-Nigeria

Sir, the hunger and the burning to change my world have been eaten me up lately. Thank God for coming across your book "CHANGING YOUR WORLD" it's a booster.

Thanks.

-Michael A.

Lagos-Nigeria.